CAERPHILLY COUNTY

3 8030 0835

D0585134

Published by Blink Publishing
Unit 3.25 The Plaza,
535 King's Road,
Chelsea Harbour,
London, SW10 0SZ

www.blinkpublishing.co.uk
facebook.com/blinkpublishing
twitter.com/blinkpublishing

HB 978-1-910536-99-5
EB 978-1-910536-78-0

All rights reserved. No part of the publication may be reproduced, stored in a retrieval system,
transmitted or circulated in any form or by any means, electronic, mechanical, photocopying, recording
or otherwise, without prior permission in writing of the publisher.

A CIP catalogue of this book is available from the British Library.

Design by Nathan Balsom

Printed and bound by UAB Balto, Lithuania

1 3 5 7 9 10 8 6 4 2

Dogs Trust Text © Deana Selby with foreword by Jennifer Blaber
Celebrity Text © RunRagged
Text Page 125 © *Spectacles* by Sue Perkins

All images © Dogs Trust, except the following (page numbers): © Jenny Goodall (30),
© Joseph Sinclair (36), © Sacre Images (40) © 2014 Alecia Moore (46, 47),
© Anthony Mayatt (48, 51), © Andy Biggar (58), © Wendy Lovatt (67),
© Jon Boast (68, 71) © Conor McDonnell (79), © Perrie Edwards (81),
© Lexie Cataldo (82, 83), © Ben Riggott (84), © Theo Walcott (85),
© Courtesy of Lewis Hamilton © 2016 44IP Ltd. Photograph by Daniel Forrest (86),
© Daily Mail (98), © Jonathan Glynn-Smith (104), © Storm Keating (110),
© Wes Simpson Photography (114, 117), © Ryan Gosling (119)

Papers used by Blink Publishing are natural, recyclable products made from wood grown in sustainable
forests. The manufacturing processes conform to the environmental regulations of the country of origin.

Every reasonable effort has been made to trace copyright holders of material reproduced in this book,
but if any have been inadvertently overlooked the publishers would be glad to hear from them.

Blink Publishing is an imprint of the Bonnier Publishing Group
www.bonnierpublishing.co.uk

DOGS

AND THEIR *faithful* CELEBRITIES

BLINK

bringing you closer

FOREWORD

Hello and welcome to *Dogs and their Faithful Celebrities*, brought to you by Dogs Trust in celebration of our 125th year of saving dogs' lives.

On behalf of dogs past, present and future, thank you for buying this book; in so doing you are helping us to continue to be a dog's best friend.

Since 1891, Dogs Trust (formerly the National Canine Defence League), has helped all sorts of dogs, from spotty to brindle; crossbreed to pedigree; and grey muzzled senior to newborn puppy. Today we are the UK's largest dog welfare charity, caring for over 17,000 dogs a year at our 21 rehoming centres – dogs like Wizzard, Lola and Kipper, whom you're about to meet in this book.

As well as finding great new homes for dogs in need, we also help people learn how to be a good dog owner, offer simple tips to parents and teachers on how to keep children safe around dogs, and help owners to be their dog's very best friend. In fact, if it's for the benefit of dog-kind, then Dogs Trust can help!

All the dogs you're about to read about in this book are well loved by their owners, but back in 1891 a dog's life wasn't always a happy one. There were few vets, stray dogs were often dealt with cruelly and dogs were regularly muzzled and tied up for long periods of time.

Thankfully, Lady Gertrude Stock, a socialite, showed the way forward by forming the National Canine Defence League in 1891, dedicated to 'Protect dogs from torture and ill usage of every kind'.

At first, the League organised public protests against laws which they felt were bad for dogs' well-being. We then opened our first shelters for stray dogs, helped poorer dog owners by paying their dog licence fee and opened up low cost vet clinics. We also campaigned against the use of dogs as circus performers. During the First and Second World Wars, we found homes for dogs who had helped with the war effort, and produced thousands of doggy gas masks.

In the 1960s we vowed we would never put a healthy dog to sleep – and we are proud to say our non-destruction policy is still very much at the heart of everything we do today.

In 1978, shocked by the huge number of dogs abandoned soon after having been given as Christmas presents, we created our now world-famous slogan, 'A dog is for life, not just for Christmas'.

In 2003 we changed our name to Dogs Trust, and, although our new name reflects the modern age, our Victorian founder's values – love and respect for all dogs – remain the foundation upon which all of our activities are built.

Today we face so many new challenges, not least the great ease with which people can buy a dog online at the click of a button, with little thought of how they will care for it. Indeed, my own dog, Skipper, whom I rehomed from our Shrewsbury centre, had originally been bought online and given as a gift, only to have been abandoned just a few days later.

Everything we have achieved over the past 125 years has only been made possible by the wonderful generosity of dog lovers just like you. As I hope you will see in our book, the bond between humans and dogs is something very special – and something for which we will continue to fight. As long as dogs need us, Dogs Trust will be around.

So thank you – and enjoy our book!

Adrian Burder
Dogs Trust Chief Executive

WIZZARD

(DOGS TRUST CANTERBURY)

Bewitching Wizzard was one of four long-legged Lurcher puppies found crammed into a cat carrying crate a week before Christmas. They were only discovered when a man who was collecting holly to make a wreath spotted the unusual object in a lay-by beside the woods.

Amazed by its unusual contents, the holly harvester took the crate straight to Dogs Trust Canterbury Rehoming Centre. There, our dedicated staff gently coaxed the shy puppies out of their cramped crate, and gave them a thorough check over. Thankfully it seems that none of the pups had been harmed, although they were very frightened by their ordeal.

Harriet, assistant manager at Dogs Trust Canterbury, explains,

'When we opened the box we saw we had two boys and two girls, and we thought they looked to be around eight weeks old. Although they were in decent condition they appeared to be simply terrified of people. It took them around a week before they felt able to come up to their canine carers for some affection.'

The boys, named Wizzard and Slade, and the girls, Buble and Bing, looked like Lurcher/Saluki crosses, and thanks to the care and patience of Team Dogs Trust, all four eventually shook off their shyness. Wizzard was the last to be rehomed, with the Hudson-Peacock family, who changed his name to Oakley.

Adam Levy, manager of Dogs Trust Canterbury, says,

'We suspect Bing, Buble, Wizzard and Slade may have been bred for the Christmas market, and then dumped when their owner realised the work involved in looking after puppies. Here at Dogs Trust we look after thousands of abandoned and unwanted dogs every year, but it still shocks us to think that someone could so callously abandon puppies.

'This year is the 38th anniversary of Dogs Trust's iconic slogan "A dog is for life, not just for Christmas" and sadly it's as true today as when it was first coined. Every year we see so many dogs handed into our rehoming centres in the days and weeks following Christmas when the appeal of a cute puppy has worn off.'

Oakley's new owner, Sheridan Hudson-Peacock, tells us,

'Oakley was a nervous puppy when we first got him, and he still has moments when he gets a bit apprehensive. We are mindful of the unhappy start to his young life, but he is improving all the time, with walks in the woods and trips out in the car to the beach and to puppy classes.'

'He also enjoys a game of "tug of war" at home and when he gets tired of all the playing he loves lying in front of the wood burner. He has quickly become an important member of our family.'

Wizzard and one of his siblings

LOLA
(DOGS TRUST LEEDS)

One frosty day in early January, Lucy, a dog control officer for Harrogate, received a call from a woman, asking that she collect a stray dog which had been abandoned in a scrap yard in Leeds.

On Lucy's arrival, the woman explained that she already had two dogs of her own and was not in a position to keep the puppy. At which point, a young Lurcher bounded up to Lucy, tail wagging and obviously delighted to meet the new visitor.

The woman explained that her daughter's boyfriend worked at a scrap metal yard, and he'd rung that morning, saying that a man had brought in his car for crushing. The yard worker had opened the boot and to his utter astonishment was greeted by the sight of a small puppy, curled up and snoozing in the corner.

He asked the customer, 'Do you realise you've left your dog in the boot?' The man apparently replied that he wanted the dog to be crushed, saying that it was either that or he would dump her on the moors.

Leaving the yard worker speechless, the customer promptly ran out of the scrap yard. The yard worker checked the dozing pup was unharmed and brought her into his office. He could see that, although quite young, the pup was unscathed by her narrow escape.

Lucy was shocked by the callousness of the pup's owner. Satisfied that this was indeed a case of abandonment, Lucy called Dogs Trust Leeds to let them know they'd soon be bringing in a very special pup for rehoming.

Meeting the dog wardens on arrival, assistant manager Emma was struck by the friendliness of the young Lurcher who bounded out of their van. Emma explains,

'She was just one of those dogs that made you smile.'

The staff named her Lola, and she proved to be a delightful dog while in the care of Dogs Trust Leeds, frolicking joyfully with her fellow puppies in the centre's 'Puppy Playground'. She'd only been at Dogs Trust three days before she was snapped up by Scott and Sarah from Dewsbury, who were instantly smitten by her friendly, chirpy nature.

Says Scott,

'Once she'd bounced out of her kennel to greet us, well, that was it! We took her for a walk, fed her a few treats, and then we knew 'This is the dog for us!'

Fast forward six weeks, and Lola is now very happily settled down into her new life.

Scott tells us,

'Lola is a really lovely, friendly dog, who gets along well with everyone, even our three cats. She's doing well at her puppy training class, is very well socialised and loves to crunch a pig's ear as a treat. She gets along brilliantly with our kids. Just thinking about what might have happened to her is awful.'

Lola

SHELBY
(DOGS TRUST MANCHESTER)

To look at Shelby the Springer Spaniel bounce around the room with her nose down and ever-wagging tail up, you'd never guess that this glossy ball of energy had been a stray just a few months prior.

Originally found wandering in Cumbria, then rehomed via Dogs Trust Manchester, this energetic youngster is now a fully licenced member of the Avon and Somerset police force. She works alongside her devoted handler, PC Ian Grant, as an explosives detection dog.

Soon after she'd arrived at Dogs Trust Manchester, Shelby was spotted by one of the canine carers, Corinna. She called assistant manager Carol over to check out the endlessly energetic Spaniel zooming around the outdoor exercise area. Carol, who had served in the army as a search dog trainer for ten years prior to working for Dogs Trust, was used to spotting dogs with the potential to excel in a working home – and Shelby clearly had that special something.

As Carol explains,

'Some dogs just shout "work me!" – and Shelby shouted it out loud!'

At Dogs Trust, we go all out to ensure that our dogs get the very best home for their needs – whether it be as a pet in a family home, or as a working dog in the armed forces, customs or prison service. When it comes to rehoming there simply can't be a 'one size fits all' policy. For Shelby, being rehomed into a working home seemed to be the very best idea for a dog with her love of playing and retrieving.

Carol started off by playing game after game of fetch with Shelby, and she could immediately see that the spaniel had a huge desire to retrieve toys which she'd carefully placed about the training area. Carol's experience told her that the toy-crazy Spaniel showed huge potential as a search dog.

The Dogs Trust Team contacted Inspector Dave Eddy, Head of Dogs for Tri-Force Specialist Operations (Wiltshire, Avon and Somerset, Gloucestershire), who came and met Shelby. On seeing her, Inspector Eddy knew she had 'it'. He also knew that PC Ian Grant, of the Avon and Somerset Constabulary, was on the lookout for a young dog to train, as his older search dog was due to retire from working life.

After meeting Shelby at Dogs Trust Manchester, Ian rehomed her and drove her back home to Somerset. Her very first task was to meet the other VID* in Ian's life, Berkeley, his other police dog. They hit it off straight away. Police search dog training for Shelby began in October, and Ian noted with pride just how quickly Shelby seemed to grasp everything that was asked of her.

As he explains,

'Shelby was born to search! There were eight other dogs on our training course but Shelby was far and away the best. Of course, to her it's all one great big game.'

Shelby passed her training in December, and since then she, Ian and Berkeley have formed a close-knit team. As a working police dog, Shelby will have to be tested in order to renew her licence for search work every 12 months.

As Ian explains,

'One of Shelby's main duties is to search buildings, routes and vehicles in advance of a visit from a VIP, for instance, the Prime Minister. Her job is to go in and check all of the building, and then we have to secure it until the visit. Shelby's role is vitally important in ensuring this country's security.'

However, life's not all work for Shelby, as she lives at home with Ian when she is off duty. He assures us that Shelby likes nothing better than rolling in muddy puddles, swimming in ponds, getting as mucky as possible and playing with her tennis balls — but she especially enjoys playing with Ian's three children.

*Very Important Dog

KIPPER AND TROOPER
(DOGS TRUST WEST LONDON)

Not-so-chipper Kipper the English Bulldog has a sweet face and adorably klutzy nature that make her a big hit with all of the team at Dogs Trust West London.

You could be forgiven for thinking that she was born this way, but nothing could be further from the truth. For Kipper is a true survivor, having overcome a traumatic start to life which tragically proved too much for two of her siblings.

Kipper and her brothers Biff, Trooper and Flappy were illegally smuggled into Britain. They'd been bred in Slovakia to be sold in the UK, to satisfy the British public's ever-increasing demand for cute puppies. At eight weeks old they had been placed in a small box and driven across Europe, before eventually arriving in Dover.

There, port officials uncovered the illegal pups, together with their smuggler, who had been hoping to slip through by carrying forged pet passports, including fake proofs of vaccination. The unlucky pups were then taken to quarantine kennels.

Sadly, Kipper is just one of thousands of young pups subjected to this incredible upheaval. Dogs Trust has been investigating the puppy smuggling scandal, where tiny pups are being smuggled into the UK by ruthless teams from Eastern Europe. The smugglers sneak pups into Britain using the Pet Travel Scheme; which was created to help people take their pets on holiday, but sadly is prone to being abused by those with an eye for a fast buck and zero interest in dog welfare.

Dogs Trust is putting pressure on the government to bring an end to the cruel trade of puppy smuggling. We also work closely with quarantine kennels at Dover so that any smuggled pups caught out by the system can quickly get vet care if needed, and will be rehomed via a Dogs Trust centre on completion of quarantine.

Tragically, two of Kipper's littermates, Flappy and Biff, did not survive their ordeal. The surviving pups, Kipper and Trooper, were transferred from the quarantine kennel (once they were 15 weeks old) to Dogs Trust West London for plenty of TLC and to eventually find new homes with loving owners.

As West London manager, Richard Moore, recalls,

'We'd cared for young puppies straight out of quarantine before, but these ones appeared to be weaker than the smuggled pups we'd previously taken in.'

All eyes were now anxiously fixed on Kipper and Trooper. As Richard explains,

'It's a nerve-wracking time for all of us. The worst part of it is that Flappy and Biff should not have died. If just a few weeks ago, a person hadn't bought a Bulldog puppy online because he was cheap, this litter would not have been bred to order, wrenched away from mum, made to travel hundreds of miles in a box, and then two of them died miserably. It makes me so angry to think how their pain could have been avoided.'

Kipper remains in the centre's isolation kennel, and as soon as she is given the all-clear by the vet, will be going home with Dogs Trust canine carer Adam, who has fallen for her. As Richard says,

'Kipper is a sweetheart and has stolen the heart of all of the staff here! Once she is strong enough to head home with Adam that will be a really happy ending to a sorry tale.'

Meanwhile, her brother, Trooper, is making slow but steady progress at the vet, and Richard hopes he'll be fit enough to find a new home very soon.

Trooper!

How did that cat get in this book?

Just a few minutes longer

Suprise!

ROXY
(DOGS TRUST LEEDS)

They say that a dog is a child's best friend, and nowhere is this more evident than in the wonderful partnership between Roxy and Sophie.

Sophie, 11, has Asperger's syndrome, which can make life lonely, especially for a child. An autistic spectrum disorder, Asperger's syndrome makes communication difficult, and often leads to anxiety attacks and a sense of isolation, among other symptoms. Roxy, three, is a quiet, calm Jack Russell Terrier cross who instinctively knows when Sophie needs her by her side.

Back in November 2013, Sophie's parents, Kat and Simon, decided to take the plunge and get a dog. Having owned rescue dogs all her adult life, Kat knew that Dogs Trust was the very best place to start their search. With two children, Sophie and her sister Lucie, and two cats in the family, Kat and Simon were keen to get the right kind of dog to fit in with their busy lifestyle.

Following a browse on the Dogs Trust website, the family decided to pop in to Dogs Trust Leeds to have a thorough look around. Kat fell for an adult dog, but unfortunately his kennel notes said he was unlikely to get along with cats or children, so they continued looking around.

Luckily, one of the centre's canine carers suggested that, given their circumstances, they might like to consider getting a puppy – a litter of three stray Jack Russell crosses having recently arrived at the centre.

Although she'd been thinking of rehoming an adult dog, Kat couldn't resist a look at the new litter, and as she says,

'Once we'd seen the Terrier pups there was no turning back. Roxy was the quietest of the trio, so we reserved her.'

As she was only six weeks old, Roxy was still being bottle fed by the Leeds canine carer team, so Kat had to wait a short while for her to be old enough to leave the centre. Eager to get Roxy off to a flying start with her new family, Dogs Trust Leeds manager Amanda suggested Kat visit the centre a few times, bringing her children, and also her cats' blankets, to help Roxy get used to the scents of her imminent new home. It was this care and attention, says Kat, which proved so helpful in settling Roxy into family life without a hitch.

Once in her new home, it took Roxy and Sophie no time at all to bond. As Kat explains,

'I've always owned dogs, and it was important to me that animals be a part of my children's lives. Sophie just seemed to be so much happier whenever Roxy was around. I could see an immediate change.

'Asperger's is a much misunderstood condition. Part of Sophie's condition is that she finds it difficult to communicate what she is feeling. Since Roxy arrived, she has found it far easier. She finds it easier to talk to the animals.'

Right from the start, Kat was keen to ensure Roxy was a part of Sophie's life. Roxy and Sophie became regulars at a local dog agility class, with Sophie accompanying her mum to sessions last summer. Kat explains,

'Like many people with Asperger's, Sophie finds routines helpful. I made sure to include stroking, feeding and talking to Roxy a part of her daily routine.'

Roxy has also been able to help Sophie feel calmer when she is out and about. As Kat explains,

'Roxy has always been good at walking nicely on the lead without pulling, and having Roxy with us when we're out reduces Sophie's anxiety level. Sometimes being out in busy places makes Sophie lose concentration, but having Roxy on her lead helps her to remain focussed.'

Sophie accompanies Roxy to her weekly agility training sessions. Kat says that Roxy is very willing to learn, and because of her enthusiasm, Sophie really enjoys taking an active role in her training. Most recently, Sophie has taught Roxy how to jump through her arms when held out in a hoop shape.

One of the effects of Sophie's condition is that, from time to time, she can become extremely stressed and very emotional. Kat is currently training Roxy to calm Sophie down from this highly stressed state by teaching her to rest her head on Sophie's lap. The simple act of stroking her beloved dog makes Sophie feel calmer. Kat reports that as Roxy is so willing to learn, training is progressing well.

Kat explains,

'Roxy has a really special bond with both Sophie and Lucie, she loves spending time with them both, and she goes to each child every day for a cuddle. She has created wonderful memories for us all as a family; we feel really lucky to have her in our lives.'

The final word must, of course, go to Sophie herself, who says,

'I like Roxy because she is always there for me and makes me happy. Roxy makes me laugh.'

Roxy's friendship has been life changing for Sophie – and with your help, Dogs Trust can continue to place dogs like Roxy with people like Sophie.

Lets play!

Roxy

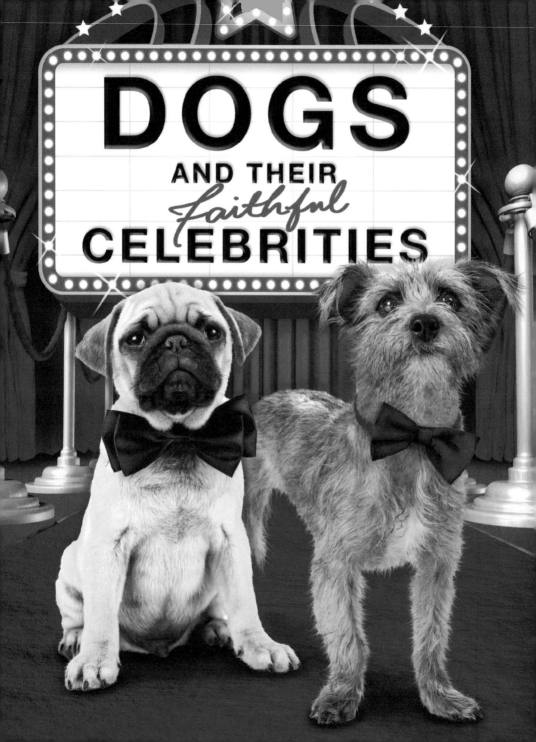

ANGELA GRIFFIN
ACTRESS AND TELEVISION PRESENTER
DOG'S NAME: **SMITH**
BREED: **CAVAPOO**

Here's me and my Cavapoo 'Smith', the doggy-love of my life.

What's the naughtiest thing your dog has ever done?
The naughtiest thing Smith has ever done is eat my husband's £250 Prada glasses whilst he was in the shower.

Which actor could provide your dog a voice and why?
I think Ricky Gervais would be ace for his voice-over because he's the perfect Reading pooch.

Smith and Angela

ANNABEL KARMEL
AUTHOR

DOG'S NAME: **HAMILTON**
BREED: **SAMOYED**

What is one of your first memories of your dog?
I will never forget when Hamilton was dognapped in Hampstead, London, when I was away and he was with a dog walker. I offered a reward and the police spent a whole day looking for him but, after ten days with no word of his whereabouts, I was getting desperate. I was lucky, however, as someone did come forward and he was returned to me, but I will never really know where he was except the police did investigate and evidently he was stolen by a known armed robber. I will always remember how happy I was and how excited he was when we were reunited.

What is the most cringeworthy 'oh no' moment?
I took my three dogs, including Sabre my Golden Retriever and Bono my American Cocker Spaniel, to Woolley Grange Hotel in the Cotswolds. When Hamilton saw the grounds he jumped out of the car and ran across the lawn straight into a lily pond not realising it was water. He then sank and eventually managed to poke his head above the surface completely covered in thick, green weeds. We had to help drag him out and his previously white thick fur was soaking wet. The smartly dressed hotel manager came out to greet us and Hamilton shook his fur, as dogs do, and completely soaked him.

ARLENE PHILLIPS

CHOREOGRAPHER, THEATRE DIRECTOR, TELEVISION JUDGE, PRESENTER AND FORMER DANCER

DOG'S NAME: LILY (SHE'S MY DAUGHTER ALANA'S PUPPY)
BREED: UNKNOWN (RESCUE PUPPY FROM CYPRUS)
AGE: SHE IS 5 MONTHS OLD
FAVOURITE TOY: HER SQEAKY DOUGHNUT!

If you could describe your dog in three words, what would they be and why?
She is snuggly, loving and playful.

What is one of your first memories of your dog?
My first memory is her leaping from her transport crate straight into my arms and just licking me all over with such excitement. She was so trusting and just so happy to have a home and someone to snuggle with.

What's the naughtiest thing your dog has ever done?
The naughtiest deed was stealing real doughnuts off the table when we went round to Alana's for tea.

Has your dog ever had any diva moments?
She's definitely a diva with her food…

What is the most cringeworthy 'oh no' moment?
I think we're still waiting for a cringe moment, but she's had a few 'oh no, Lily!' accidents with her toilet training!

Which actor could provide your dog a voice and why?
Her celebrity voice would definitely be by Mila Kunis.

ASHLEIGH BUTLER

DOG TRAINER AND WINNER OF BRITAIN'S GOT TALENT

DOG'S NAME: PUDSEY
BREED: BORDER COLLIE, CHINESE CRESTED POWDERPUFF AND BICHON FRISE CROSS

If you could describe your dog in three words, what would they be and why?
1. Greedy, because he is obsessed by food! Anything he can get his hands on, he will try!
2. Performer, because he just loves to show off. When he's performing, the more the audience cheer for him the more he shows off!
3. Lazy, because Pudsey loves his sleep, and when he's not performing or showing off, he loves to go for a good nap!

What is one of your first memories of your dog?
Pudsey was a very naughty puppy, and he loved toys. One day he decided my younger sister's hair in a plait looked like the best toy ever, and decided to tug on it and wouldn't let go.

What's the naughtiest thing your dog has ever done?
He once jumped over a gate and then jumped up onto our kitchen work surfaces and started to steal some food. My mum caught him in the act and he had a very guilty look on his face!

Has your dog ever had any diva moments?
Pudsey has still got his paws firmly on the ground, but the quality of his treats has definitely gone up! He doesn't like boring dog treats any more, he wants ham sandwiches and steak!

What is the most cringeworthy 'oh no' moment?
The night we won *Britain's Got Talent* I took Pudsey out for a wee and he was papped mid flow! He was not happy.

Which actor could provide your dog a voice and why?
David Walliams was kind enough to provide Pudsey his voice in the movie we made. I think he did a brilliant job, and I couldn't imagine anyone else doing it.

ASHLEY ROBERTS

SINGER, SONGWRITER, CHOREOGRAPHER, ACTRESS, MODEL AND TELEVISION PRESENTER

DOG'S NAME: **COOPER**
BREED: **MALTESE**

If you could describe your dog in three words, what would they be and why?
1. Ninja – because he is an escape artist. He climbed out of his play pen when he was a pup.
2. Independent – he gives cuddles on his own terms.
3. Cool – he's a small dude but so cool. He knows he's a badass.

What is one of your first memories of your dog?
I was meant to look at two other puppies and he was the first. I asked him if he wanted to come home with me. He sat between my legs and looked up at me. That was it. The two of us left right after that.

Which actor could provide your dog a voice and why?
I think his voice would be like Simba in *The Lion King*, or Ryan Reynolds.

BEN FOGLE
ADVENTURER, AUTHOR, BROADCASTER AND WRITER

DOG'S NAME: **STORM**
BREED: **LABRADOR**
FAVOURITE TOYS: **FOOD OVER TOYS EVERY TIME**

If you could describe your dog in three words, what would they be and why?
Funny, loyal and happy because she is all of those things. She loves us and we love her. She brings optimism and happiness into our lives.

What is one of your first memories of your dog?
I remember my first dog, Liberty (a golden retriever), digging for stones in a small stream near our home in Sussex. She would stick her whole face in the water and blow bubbles through her nose. I used to stare in amazement at how long she could stay underwater.

What's the naughtiest thing your dog has ever done?
Too many to count, as I have had Labradors for the last 15 years. It usually involves food. Storm stole my mother-in-law's Sunday roast ham. She also stole the children's chicken, some banana bread, the butter dish...

Have the dogs ever had any diva moments?
On the contrary, Storm loves the camera. She is quite at home in front of the lens.

What is the most cringeworthy 'oh no' moment?
When she ate her own poo.

Which actor could provide your dog a voice and why?
Taylor Swift.

CAMILLA DALLERUP
BALLROOM DANCER, LIFE COACH AND AUTHOR

DOG'S NAME: **SVEN**
BREED: **A STAFFIE AND AN ENGLISH BULL TERRIER CROSSED WITH A BIT OF PARSON JACK RUSSELL TERRIER**
AGE: **9**
FAVOURITE TOY: **HIS DUCKIE AND HIS BASEBALLS**

(THE PHOTO WAS TAKEN AT A PARK IN LOS ANGELES)

If you could describe your dog in three words, what would they be and why?
Loving, loyal and present.

What is one of your first memories of your dog?
The very first time I met Sven was when we were filming *The Underdog Show* at Dog Trust and all the celebrities were paired up with different rescue dogs. I met Sven and my now husband for the first time together as Kevin had chosen Sven to be his dog on the show. I remember thinking bless that little dog he looks so sad and scruffy and in real need of some love. Well I didn't need to worry because Kevin fell in love with Sven immediately and then we fell in love and the rest, as they say, is history. Sven is such an important link in our love story and I'm so grateful that Kevin decided to adopt him after the show.

What's the naughtiest thing your dog has ever done?
A few weeks after Kevin adopted him he was on his own in my apartment for a bit and somehow had looked out the window and caught his paw in the blinds and pulled them down. I presume he then tried to chew a bit off the bottom of them to get himself unstuck. It looked a right mess when we got in but we soon realised it was an accident. He did, however, chew my husband's favourite designer shoes too, which I believe was no accident!

Has the dog ever had any diva moments?
Actually he is pretty good, except if we have travelled and been away, he will run up and say hi and then he will snub us for a day or so. He is not too happy when the suitcases come out.

What is the most cringeworthy 'oh no' moment?
It's a tough call. It could be the day he rolled himself in fox poo, it smelled so bad and I had to get in a lift to get to my apartment. I remember thinking please, please let there be no one in the lift with me, but of course there had to be and they kept looking at me like 'do something'. Or it could be when we first moved to LA and we had to go to see a friend who was staying in this amazing house in the hills and said to bring Sven along. This house was stunning and full of beautiful sculptures and huge crystals and we had to enter the house to get through to the pool area and patio where the dogs could run around. As we entered the house, Sven ran straight up to pee on the most stunning amethyst crystal stood on the floor. He never ever does that inside so I was mortified having to say hello to the owner of the house for the first time and ask for tissues to clean up the mess all in one sentence.

Which actor could provide your dog a voice and why?
My husband, Kevin Sacre, does the best voice for Sven as he truly captures his huge personality.

ALFIE DEYES
VLOGGER

DOG'S NAME: **NALA**   BREED: **PUG**

If you could describe your dog in three words, what would they be and why?
Cute, lovable and nutty.

What is one of your first memories of your dog?
Seeing Nala all excited running upstairs and then, two minutes later, having a little cry as she was too scared to walk back down.

Has your dog ever had any diva moments?
Every day over everything!

CHER LLOYD
SINGER

DOGS' NAMES: SHARON ($4\frac{1}{2}$) AND BUDDY ($3\frac{1}{2}$)
BREED: (SHARON) WHITE ENGLISH BULLDOG AND (BUDDY) BLACK FRENCH BULLDOG

If you could describe your dogs in three words, what would they be and why?
Friendly – They both want to be involved in everything. They love meeting new people and being fussed over.
Loving – Sharon likes to rest her head on your shoulder and Buddy likes to sit on your lap. They are both extremely loving.
Funny – They are always making me laugh. Sharon doesn't shake her tail she shakes her whole backside!

What is one of your first memories of your dogs?
When Buddy got his first toy. It was a stuffed skunk and he carried it everywhere! I remember Sharon as a puppy and how she was so shy! But it didn't take her long to come out of her shell!

What's the naughtiest thing your dogs have ever done?
Sharon once chewed through a pair of my favourite shoes!

Have your dogs ever had any diva moments?
Every day! When we're out on a walk Sharon likes to lay out flat and refuse to move. She's a little stubborn sometimes!

What is the most cringeworthy 'oh no' moment?
My mum had just planted some flowers and Buddy dug all of them up!

CAREY HART

FREESTYLE MOTOCROSS,
MOTORCYCLE RACER

DOG'S NAME: **LUCKY**
BREED: **AMERICAN STAFFORDSHIRE BULL TERRIER**

PINK
SINGER, SONGWRITER,
DANCER AND ACTRESS

This is Lucky and he's an American Staffordshire that had parvo when Pink and Carey rescued him from the high-kill San Bernardino Shelter. He was only nine weeks old at the time. Pink and Willow (Pink and Carey's daughter) visited him in the hospital until he got better and now he's living the life as the most loving 65lb lap dog!

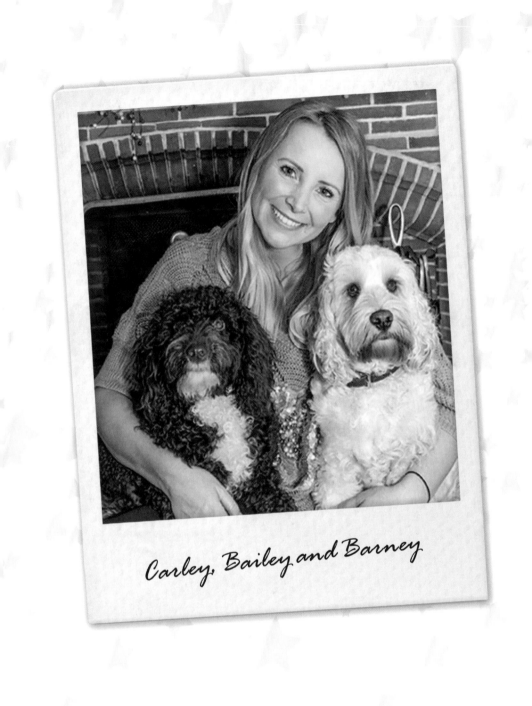

Carley, Bailey and Barney

CARLEY STENSON
ACTRESS AND SINGER

DOGS' NAMES: **BAILEY (LEFT) AND BARNEY (RIGHT)**
BREED: **COCKERPOOS**

If you could describe your dogs in three words, what would they be and why?
Barney: Funny, grumpy and gorgeous.
Bailey: Mad, snuggley and cute.

What is one of your first memories of your dogs?
Barney: Watching the video back after we filmed him with all his brothers and sisters. Deciding which one we were going to pick as we really couldn't decide. Then seeing this little one with a heart-shaped patch on his head try to get my attention from the rest with his paw on my foot. THAT'S OUR BOY.

Bailey: He was the quiet one who just sat on my knee the whole time while his brother played. I thought this one needs a calm home with lots of love... little did I know he had us fooled and is the craziest dog we've ever known.

What's the naughtiest thing your dogs have ever done?
Barney's not really naughty. Just a stubborn teenager and won't come back when shouted sometimes because he knows best and would rather chase a bird or discover what's in the lake. After his bath he will then need one again in five minutes. It's like he does it on purpose.

Bailey is a little tinker though haha. Aw no, he's not really but he did eat the Christmas decoration and we found out his brother did the same thing in another home. Bailey just barks at you for no reason and we are sure he thinks he's telling us off for at least a good three minutes. Then he just goes back to sleep whilst we are left confused.

Have your dogs ever had any diva moments?
Barney is a diva when he wants to be left alone. He does this grumpy little moan and looks at you without lifting his head as if to say 'you're doing my head in' haha. **Bailey**'s barking rant is very diva ish although he's wagging his tail. It's almost as if he ends on 'and that's that!' before he just goes back to sleep.

Barney loves getting dirty, whereas Bailey avoids mess. The thing is, Barney is the apricot colour so it's more obvious. Whenever we go for a walk we're always apologising if he brushes up against someone or they can smell him coming. But his face is a picture. It's when he's happiest!

Which actor could provide your dogs a voice and why?
Barney would have a grounded, slower, older voice like James Earl Jones.
Bailey would have a high pitched, erratic, child-like voice like Bart Simpson.

CAROLINE QUENTIN

ACTRESS

DOGS' NAMES:
QUEENIE AND FIFI
BREED: QUEENIE IS A SPANIEL COLLIE CROSS (BROWN AND WHITE) AND FIFI IS A MALTESE TERRIER (SMALL AND WHITE) THAT MY MUM BEQUEATHED TO ME IN HER WILL

If you could describe your dogs in three words, what would be and why?
Dim and dimmer. Queenie stares at the hens ALL DAY if I let her, the chickens don't mind but it drives me crazy.

What's the naughtiest thing your dogs have ever done?
When Queenie was a pup she disgraced herself on the guest bed ... As our visitor walked into the bedroom ... Lovely welcome.

Have any of your dogs ever had any diva moments?
They are both full time divas.

Which actor could provide your dogs a voice and why?
Queenie would be voiced by Joan Greenwood and Fifi by Doris Day.

CHARLOTTE HAWKINS

TELEVISION PRESENTER,
NEWSREADER AND JOURNALIST

DOG'S NAME: **BAILEY**
BREED: **TERRIER CROSS (RESCUE DOG)**
AGE: **9 YEARS OLD**
FAVOURITE TOY: **EITHER HER KONG**
OR SQEAKY TOY SQUIRREL

When we first met Bailey, the rescue centre brought her and her sister to our house so we could say hello and choose which puppy we wanted. The first thing they both did was to do a poo on our floor which was a bit of a baptism of fire for us!

What is one of your first memories of your dog?
One of my early memories of Bailey was when we let her off the lead for the first time. We were in the park and it was raining so there weren't many people around – it was nice and quiet. We let her off the lead and she ran straight into a pond that was covered in weeds, so she hadn't noticed it wasn't grass! I had to throw myself on the ground and pull her out – getting absolutely covered in pond weed and dirty water at the same time...

What's the naughtiest thing your dog has ever done?
We are lucky with Bailey as she is usually a well-behaved dog, but she was very lively as a puppy. One time I was upstairs, she found a big foam ball and within minutes had ripped it into thousands of tiny pieces. When I came downstairs it looked like it had been snowing! It took me hours to clear it all up.

Chris and Miley

CHRIS SMALLING
ENGLISH INTERNATIONAL AND PROFESSIONAL FOOTBALLER

DOG'S NAME: **MILEY**
BREED: **A CROSS BETWEEN A COCKER SPANIEL AND PARSON RUSSELL**
AGE: **6**

What is one of your first memories of your dog?
When I met Miley, she was one and she immediately jumped on me. From that day onwards she always wants to fall asleep on my lap.

What's the naughtiest thing your dog has ever done?
She had eaten an Easter egg that I had left on the hall side table. I came home to see only the wrapper. Then when we called Miley her head was just peering round the corner, which she only does when she knows she's messed up.

GEMMA ATKINSON

ACTRESS

DOG'S NAME: **NORMAN**
BREED: **SPROODLE - SPRINGER SPANIEL POODLE CROSS**

If you could describe your dog in three words, what would they be and why?
Describing Norman in three words would be 'My Best Friend'.

What's the naughtiest thing your dog has ever done?
The naughtiest thing he has done is chew holes in a new throw I bought for a guest bedroom. It took me ages to find one that matches the room and bedding and after only a week there were at least 14 holes in it! He was sneaking in there while I was at work.

Which actor could provide your dog a voice and why?
Celeb voice wise I think the late Robin Williams would have been great. He had the crazy, funny wild side to his voice but also that soft, gentle side and Norman has all those qualities.

Bettie and Heidi

HEIDI RANGE
SINGER AND SONGWRITER

DOG'S NAME: **BETTIE**
BREED: **PUG**

If you could describe your dog in three words, what would they be and why?
Crazy, loving and snuggly.

What is one of your first memories of your dog?
The first time I met B she was sitting in the palm of my sister Hayley's hand. She was so tiny and adorable, it was love at first sight!

What's the naughtiest thing your dog has ever done?
Destroyed my designer sofa!

Has the dog ever had any diva moments?
B has diva moments on a daily basis. She gets particularly upset when she sees other dogs on TV; she just doesn't understand why they got the gig over her. She also has a massive problem with the confused.com advert!

What is the most cringeworthy 'oh no' moment?
Bettie has recently picked a new favourite spot to do her daily business, half way up the steps at the tube station, often conveniently during rush hour. Sorry fellow commuters!

JACQUIE BELTRAO
SPORTS PRESENTER AND
FORMER OLYMPIC GYMNAST

DOG'S NAME: TEDDY
BREED: BICHON/ JACK RUSSELL CROSS

If you could describe your dog in three words, what would they be and why?
Sweet little bear.

What is one of your first memories of your dog?
My first memory was seeing him in the puppy area at Dogs Trust. We'd brought Maddie, our other Dogs Trust dog, to meet him and he got so excited, he was doing roly-polys jumping all over us and licking our faces. We couldn't not choose him after that!

What's the naughtiest thing your dog has ever done?
His naughty moments involve flip-flops; he chews through the toe part making them useless – he's done this to quite a few pairs!

Has your dog ever had any diva moments?
He's never had a proper diva moment but he has had a 'Fenton' moment chasing deer in Richmond Park. He wouldn't stop – no matter how much I shouted he just kept running – it was very bad. He also likes to sleep under the duvet, which is pretty diva-ish, I guess.

Which actor could provide your dog a voice and why?
Who would play him in a movie? A young Macaulay Culkin.

JAMES HASKELL

ENGLISH INTERNATIONAL
RUGBY UNION PLAYER

DOG'S NAME: **AERO**
BREED: **LABRADOR WEIMARANER CROSS**

If you could describe your dog in three words, what would they be and why?
Clever, energetic and affectionate.

What is one of your first memories of your dog?
The first night I got him, he barked the place down, ate a tub of protein powder, and smashed a jar of fish oils apart, eating half of them in the process and cutting his mouth.

What's the naughtiest thing your dog has ever done?
Taken a whole Christmas ham off the work top and tried to run out the house with it.

Has your dog ever had any diva moments?
Yes, all the time. He only plays on his terms, or he goes back to the house. If you don't give him attention he jumps on you.

What is the most cringeworthy 'oh no' moment?
The first time I took him into Wasps after having him for five days. He did a massive liquid poo in the middle of the corridor outside the changing room. All the lads were gagging.

Which actor could provide your dog a voice and why?
Very good question. Aero is a bit old, a bit wise, kind of camp and a bit of a know-it-all. He is also quite posh, so maybe Sir Ian McKellen?

JAMIE CAMPBELL BOWER

ACTOR, SINGER AND MODEL

DOG'S NAME: **BAYA**
BREED: **LAKELAND TERRIER**
AGE: **6 YEARS OLD**

Which actor could provide your dog a voice and why?
Meryl Streep would play her in a movie because she oozes class.

HAYLEY TAMADDON

ACTRESS
DOG'S NAME: **FRANKIE**
BREED: **PUG/TERRIER CROSS**

What is one of your first memories of your dog?
Picking him up from Dogs Trust... He was so excited he just weed everywhere!

What's the naughtiest thing your dog has ever done?
Pooed under the dining room table!

Which actor could provide your dog a voice and why?
My boyfriend, Joe Tracini, who is an actor often pretends to do my dogs voice...
And it's hilarious! So I choose him!

JASMINE HARMAN
TELEVISION PRESENTER

DOG'S NAME: **SHADOW**
AGE OF DOG AT TIME OF PHOTOS: **1 YEAR OLD**
BREED: **BERNESE MOUNTAIN DOG**
FAVOURITE TOY: **HIS RED MONKEY**

If you could describe your dog in three words, what would they be and why?
Cuddly – he gave the best cuddles ever, especially if I was feeling sad, he knew and he'd come and put his head under my arm for a cuddle.
Greedy – I've never met a dog so obsessed with food. He'd do anything for the tiniest morsel and we learned never to leave food on the counter. He even managed to get the fruit bowl off a high shelf a few times!
Confident – from a very young age I took Shadow everywhere with me, even on location whilst filming *A Place in the Sun*. As a result he was happy and confident in most situations.

What is one of your first memories of your dog?
His first walk was on my husband Jon's 30th birthday. Shadow was 11 weeks old, we took him to Morden Hall Park and had a little picnic. He caused quite a stir; he was just the cutest little ball of fluff! It was always his favourite place to walk and we scattered his ashes there after he died.

What's the naughtiest thing your dog has ever done?
It's hard to pick just one... But every time he was naughty, food was involved. Like the time he ate a whole unopened packet of mini Wham bars (including wrappers!) that he stole and the next day produced a purple poo!

Has the dog ever had any diva moments?
Shadow wasn't much of a diva, although when he came on location with me he had a dog-nanny to look after his every need whilst I was at work, and spent most of the day under a parasol on a sun lounger by the pool!

What is the most cringeworthy 'oh no' moment?
When we went to my cousin's wedding and he went to visit his best friend Bungle, he ate a whole apple crumble from the kitchen counter, and later emptied the entire contents of Bungle's mummy's rubbish bin (no doubt looking for food). She sent me a photo and I just wanted the Earth to swallow me!

Which actor could provide your dog a voice and why?
Richard Ridings, who plays Daddy Pig, with the personality of Doug, the dog from *Up*.

Jasmine and Shadow

JOHN PARTRIDGE
ACTOR, SINGER AND DANCER

DOG'S NAME: **WINNIE**
BREED: **JACK RUSSELL**

If you could describe your dog in three words, what would they be and why?
1. Escapologist: she can open doors!
2. Retriever: she is obsessed with playing fetch! A Labrador trapped in a Jack Russell's body…
3. Sensitive: she has a very gentle side.

What is one of your first memories of your dog?
The first memory of seeing Winnie was at Dogs Trust Canterbury. For a Jack Russell she was very quiet. She looked up at us (a look we now call her 'Lady Diana') and we knew we couldn't leave her there. The Queen of Hearts stole ours!

What's the naughtiest thing your dog has ever done?
This question could fill a book on its own! When we first brought Winnie home she was quite destructive… Arms off jackets, shutters off windows, utility rooms flooded. Yes, she not only opens doors, but turns on taps too!

Has the dog ever had any diva moments?
See above.

What is the most cringeworthy 'oh no' moment?
That would probably be me – after throwing a stick (or should I say a small tree) for Winnie to fetch only for it to smack centrally between the shoulder blades of an unsuspecting walker… Ouch!

Which actor could provide your dog a voice and why?
She's quite a tomboy, and let's not forget an Irish girl, so… let's say Mrs Brown from *Mrs Brown's Boys*.

Katarina, Bronx and Chorizo

KATARINA
JOHNSON-THOMPSON
TRACK AND FIELD ATHLETE

DOGS' NAMES: **BRONX AND CHORIZO**
BREED: **DASCHUND**

You don't realise how hard it is to get two dogs both facing the same way! The brown one is called Bronx and the black one is called Chorizo. Both boys!

You couldn't get more different personalities with them both! Every morning Bronx is so excitable whereas Chorizo is a slow starter and will stay in his bed! I love them both so much, I hate leaving them when I go away to compete!

Kate and Stella

KATE NASH
SINGER, SONGWRITER, MUSICIAN AND ACTRESS

DOG'S NAME: **STELLA**
BREED: **STELLA IS A RESCUE DOG**

If you could describe your dog in three words, what would they be and why?
Insane, lover and Olympian.

What is one of your first memories of your dog?
I don't know. I actually rescued Stella from a coffee shop in LA in Echo Park. I was getting coffee and already having a pretty peculiar day when a guy walked in and said he needed $20 to get off drugs and leave town. This dog was jumping around on a dirty rope and she was beautiful and helpless. I just sort of stared blankly and said, 'OK'. I went home, changed into dog-friendly attire, grabbed my car and the $20 and then made the exchange. Once they'd put her in my car and walked away I regretted it immediately as she was jumping like a bullet from the back to the front of the car. I felt like I'd made a mistake and was jumping into a shark tank, I didn't know this dog's behaviour and nature; what if she ripped my throat out? I started shouting around for help and miraculously a woman leaped out of her car and said, 'I rescue dogs all the time.' I looked over and there were three eager Chihuahuas in the front seat. She kindly helped me to calm Stella down and settle her safely in the car. I drove to my friend's house for help and within 20 minutes I was in love. She was curled into a ball, only eating from my hand, being ridiculously cute. I initially only intended to help her out and rescue her, and I did find her a temporary home, but the universe brought us back together when that home could no longer keep her due to landlord issues and I just thought, well, this is love. She was with me through all the scary things that happened my first year living in LA, she saw me through rough moments and is my best friend.

What's the naughtiest thing your dog has ever done?
Let me count the ways... She jumped the fence on my old place before I knew she could fly; I've seen her jump a 10 ft wall before. She doesn't get on with little dogs with attitude and will try to eat them. She'll go for anything on wheels too, and she chewed up my porch fence the day before I moved out, eating up a nice

chunk of my deposit. She once ate my dinner off the counter when I was sad and I was so annoyed with her. I also caught her standing up on the counters after she'd eaten a whole bowl of sweets. Oh also, if you put a bandana on her she will go psycho.

Has the dog ever had any diva moments?

I would say diva is the wrong word for Stella, she's way too clumsy and goofy for that word. She's always falling into things. BUT if we've had an argument, which we sometimes do, she'll get mad and we both hold resentments. She'll do stuff like turn her bed around and really make a big fuss over digging into it and getting it as far away from me as possible and turning around and sighing really loudly if she hasn't got what she wants. One time we went on a road trip when my sister was in town. She acted so nuts in this cabin in Big Bear cause she was so over excited by all the new smells, so I put her lead on her for the end of the night and kept her by me to calm her down so she wouldn't hurt herself. And she was SOOOO angry with me. I'd wanted her to sleep in the bed with me seeing as we were on holiday but she wouldn't do it and turned her bed around and I was really upset we were fighting on our first night of holiday. I was like 'Are you really gonna do that?', turned off the light and then, within five minutes, I heard her get up and come towards the bed. She wouldn't even look at me but she got into the bed and I was big spoon. I was so happy when she got in, haha.

What is the most cringeworthy 'oh no' moment?

I think when she ate the fence I was the most embarrassed. My landlord had not initially wanted me to have a dog and did me a massive favour by letting her in so I couldn't believe it when, on the last day, she totally destroyed a huge part of the garden and porch. It was really cringy having to tell him. But luckily I had the nicest landlord in the world and he was super cool about it all. But honestly every day Stella provides me with a cringeworthy moment. She'll eat too much grass and I'll have to pull it out of her arse cause she can't poop it all out, usually in front of people, in the middle of the road. The hatred of wheels is really embarrassing when you're trying to sit and have lunch and she leaps across the table spilling everything everywhere. And if someone in a wheelchair comes past I feel like I have to shout, 'My dog's not evil! It's the wheels!' She also has this desperate howly bark when she sees dogs she wants to play with. I tell her she needs to act a little cooler to make more friends.

Which actor could provide your dog a voice and why?

Maybe Pippin from *The Lord of the Rings*.

LAURA WHITMORE

TELEVISION PRESENTER

DOG'S NAME: KING OF CUTE A.K.A
MICK (JAGGER)
BREED: MALTESE AND TOY POODLE CROSS

King of Cute!!!

LEIGH-ANNE PINNOCK

SINGER

DOG'S NAME: **HARVEY**

BREED: **PUG CROSS**

AGE: **5**

Merry Christmas!

PERRIE EDWARDS

SINGER

DOG'S NAME: **HATCHI**
BREED: **POMERANIAN**
AGE: **3 AND A HALF YEARS OLD**

LESLEY NICOL

ACTRESS

DOGS' NAMES: **BERTIE (RIGHT) AND FREDDIE (LEFT)**
BREED: **BERTIE IS A TIBETAN TERRIER
AND FREDDIE IS A POODLE**

If you could describe your dogs in three words, what would they be and why?
Bertie: Show-off, dramatic and entertaining.
Freddie: Shy, joyful and loving.

What is one of your first memories of your dogs?
Freddie – when we picked him up from the rescue home – he was in a little blue polo neck sweater and he was shaking.

What's the naughtiest thing your dogs have ever done?
We were having Christmas dinner with friends – and Bertie was found standing in the middle of their beautifully laid table! Later he made it up onto the table where the desserts were! Nightmare!

LEONA LEWIS
SINGER
DOG'S NAME: **FORREST**
BREED: **CHIHUAHUA CROSS**
AGE: **4 YEARS OLD IN THIS PHOTO**
FAVOURITE TOY: **HE LIKES SQUEAKY TOYS BUT NOTHING BEATS A TREAT TO KEEP HIM HAPPY!**

THEO WALCOTT
PROFESSIONAL FOOTBALLER
DOGS' NAMES: **TYSON AND HUGO**
BREED: **TYSON (BLACK) PUG CROSSED WITH A GRIFFON. HUGO (SAND) PUG CROSSED WITH A SHIH TZU**

LEWIS HAMILTON
BRITISH FORMULA ONE RACING DRIVER

DOG'S NAME: **ROSCOE**
BREED: **BULLDOG**

LABRINTH

SINGER AND SONGWRITER

DOG'S NAME: **LAIKA**   BREED: **CHIHUAHUA**

If you could describe your dog in three words, what would they be and why?

Intelligent, nurturing and intuitive. Laika can sniff illness of any kind. And she will sit next to you and make sure you're okay.

What is one of your first memories of your dog?

She's actually not my dog. My fiancé got the dog when she was 17 as a therapy dog. She saved her life. Five years later Laika came with my fiancé from Denmark and we got on straight away, she's my girl now though.

What's the naughtiest thing your dog has ever done?

It wasn't just Laika, all our pets were involved. We had taken out some chicken from the freezer and the cat must've jumped up and thrown chicken down to our dogs. There were chicken bones everywhere!

Has your dog ever had any diva moments?

All the time…

Which actor could provide your dog a voice and why?

Eddie Murphy because he's talented and he would pull it off.

LILAH PARSONS
MODEL AND RADIO PRESENTER

DOG'S NAME: BETTY
BREED: CAVALIER

If you could describe your dog in three words, what would they be and why?
Cheeky (she understands the rules, she just chooses to ignore them!), beautiful and cuddly! (She loves nothing more than being curled up on someone's lap.)

What is one of your first memories of your dog?
When I went to visit the breeder in Connecticut (Betty is American!) she was the one out of the group of puppies that came over to me and sat on my foot! She must have been 8 weeks old.

What's the naughtiest thing your dog has ever done?
Naughtiest thing – shredding loo roll all over the house!

What is the most cringeworthy 'oh no' moment?
A cringeworthy 'oh no' is when I took her to MTV for the day. She was on great form, she even had her own little feature on my show! Then she pooed everywhere... And I mean everywhere! I was mortified.

Which actor could provide your dog a voice and why?
Elizabeth Taylor would have been perfect!

Linda and Ernie

LINDA ROBSON
ACTRESS AND PRESENTER

DOG'S NAME: **ERNIE (IN THE PICTURE)**
BREED: **FRENCH BULLDOG**

GEORGE - STAFFORDSHIRE BULL TERRIER.

George is Linda's dog that passed away. 'Animals are such a huge part of the family and George was such a huge part of ours. Staffordshire Bull Terriers get a really bad reputation but George had such a lovely personality; he was so good with the children. He had a kind and loving nature. He was even scared of our neighbours' cat!'

If you could describe your dogs in three words, what would they be and why?
George – Intelligent, loyal and loving.
Ernie – Scatty, loving and mischievous.

What is one of your first memories of your dogs?
My daughter Bobbie went to collect Ernie and she sent me a video of him with his brothers and sisters. I don't know what it was but he just stood out from the rest. I fell in love instantly.

What's the naughtiest thing your dogs have ever done?
Pooed on my bed! We have to close all the doors when we're not in so he doesn't leave me a surprise in the bedroom!

What is the most cringeworthy 'oh no' moment?
Ernie once stole our friends' baby's dummy! We took it out quick so we could sterilise it. He did look quite cute though!

Which actor could provide your dogs a voice and why?
Ernie – Rylan!
George – Russell Brand.

LORRAINE PASCALE
BRITISH TELEVISION COOK

DOG'S NAME: **WATSON**
BREED: **CROSSBREED**

If you could describe your dog in three words, what would they be and why?
Cute, playful and relaxed.

What's the naughtiest thing your dog has ever done?
He pulled a roast chicken off the table when we weren't looking.

Has the dog ever had any diva moments?
Every day he has a diva moment. He won't come when he knows I'm in a rush to get out and hides under the bed where it's impossible to reach him.

LOUIS SMITH
OLYMPIC GYMNAST

DOG'S NAME: **LUNA**
BREED: **HUSKY**
AGE: **1 YEAR OLD**

What is one of your first memories of your dog?
Going to pick her up and seeing straight away how she was too hyperactive and boisterous for other puppies, running at them and knocking them over.

What's the naughtiest thing your dog has ever done?
Rolling in fox poo and then shaking it off all over my girlfriend at the time.

Which actor could provide your dog a voice and why?
Jim Carrey.

PROFESSOR GREEN

RAPPER, SONGWRITER, ACTOR
AND TELEVISION PERSONALITY

DOG'S NAME: **ARTHUR**

BREED: **STAFFORDSHIRE BULL TERRIER**

MATTHEW WRIGHT

TELEVISION PRESENTER AND TABLOID JOURNALIST
DOG'S NAME: **WIGGY**
BREED: **SCHNAUZER**

If you could describe your dog in three words, what would they be and why?
Loyal, loving and schnuffly (it's a Schnauzer thing: from the way they schnuffle along with their beards).

What is one of your first memories of your dog?
My first memory of a dog was my nan's Skye Terrier Stella. Stella wasn't very well socialised as a puppy and consequently wasn't exactly warm and friendly, save when she was with my nan. I remember being five or six and being scared witless of going into my nan's room in case Stella went for me. She never did of course, just growled a bit!

What's the naughtiest thing your dog has ever done?
The naughtiest thing Wiggy has ever done occurred on national TV, on *The Alan Titchmarsh Show* a couple of years ago. As part of the fun we were invited to run through a mini obstacle course. Wiggy did his bit just fine, brilliantly in fact, and then decided to celebrate by peeing all over the set, everywhere. Alan was lucky he didn't get a soaking…

Has your dog ever had any diva moments?
Wiggy doesn't have diva moments, as he's a diva 24/7. He loves caviar – seriously – and nicely cooked steak. He sleeps on a ludicrously expensive bed and insists on Access All Area passes when invited to go backstage at gigs.

What is the most cringeworthy 'oh no' moment?
The most embarrassing thing Wiggy has ever done was dress up as a ballerina at a doggy fun day. It was done as a tribute to the movie *Black Swan* but the look did nothing for his street cred.

Which actor could provide your dog a voice and why?
The late, great Alan Rickman would have been perfect; his mellifluous tones would have suited a classy mutt like Wiggy just fine.

MICHAEL BALL
SINGER AND ACTOR

DOGS' NAMES: FREDDIE (PICTURED) AND OLLIE
BREED: TIBETAN TERRIER

If you could describe your dogs in three words, what would they be and why?
Freddie: Bloody minded, brave and deaf.
Ollie: Affectionate, needy and lovable.

What is one of your first memories of your dogs?
Freddie: Refusing to settle until he could sleep in the bedroom, howling the house down!
Ollie: Getting him home for the first time, sitting him on my lap on my chair and him falling asleep.

What's the naughtiest thing your dogs have ever done?
Freddie: Refusing to come back after following a girl dog for over a mile!
Ollie: Getting into the sitting room and tearing open all the Christmas presents! Total carnage!

Have your dogs ever had any diva moments?
Freddie: His life is one long diva moment…
Ollie: Always sulks for a day when he comes back from staying with his best friends Woody and Chudley the Great Danes

Which actor could provide your dogs a voice and why?
Freddie: The late Alan Rickman. Aloof, slightly superior with a naughty sense of humour.
Ollie: Maybe me? We're soul mates.

NATHALIE EMMANUEL
ACTRESS

DOG'S NAME: **DRAKE**
BREED: **LHASA APSO**

If you could describe your dog in three words, what would they be and why?
A bit mental!

What is one of your first memories of your dog?
When I met him he was fascinated by my curly hair so, naturally, he decided to chew it... and it was then that I realised he was supposed to be my dog...

What's the naughtiest thing your dog has ever done?
He climbed into a bin bag and ate an out-of-date beef stroganoff. You'd think because that incident made him sick he would have learnt his lesson... but no. Food stealing, in general, seems to be a pattern. We call him 'the cheese burglar' because he really likes cheese and I won't give it to him, so I guess he just does what he has to do to get it. I have to respect his determination really.

Has your dog ever had any diva moments?
His general lack of enthusiasm to walk is a good place to start. We walk him every day but he'd much rather sleep. He will just lie down when he has had enough so we have to encourage him a little so that he gets enough exercise.

What is the most cringeworthy 'oh no' moment?
Well he has pooed in a few major train stations in the UK... London Euston, Liverpool Lime Street, Manchester Piccadilly... I think even Birmingham International too... Pretty embarrassing picking up poo as disapproving commuters walk past...

Which actor could provide your dog a voice and why?
Liam Neeson – his Aslan voice from *The Lion, the Witch and the Wardrobe* specifically – I think it just fits Drake's appearance. Also, I feel like Drake is an old soul. His big brown eyes feel wise, like he has seen many things and has many tales to tell.

"Stop taking photos and
go to sleep, Ollie !"

OLLIE LOCKE
REALITY TV STAR

DOG'S NAME: **BEAR**
BREED: **POMERANIAN CROSSED WITH A CHIHUAHUA, OR A POM-CHI**

What is one of your first memories of your dog?
When I walked in to get Bear at 17 weeks old as a family couldn't have him any more. I walked in and said, 'Herro', I picked him up and he put both paws on my eyes. And I said, 'You had me at herro!'

What's the naughtiest thing your dog has ever done?
Bear is constantly naughty; he is known as the ninja, as he steals everything and looks innocent! He seems to have an infatuation with cake, if someone brings cake into the house he will do anything to find a way to get to that cake and this happens frequently!

Which actor could provide your dog a voice and why?
Being someone known for a posh accent, I feel that Bear would absolutely be voiced by Danny Dyer. It would just confuse people and make dog walks even more wonderful!

PATRICK COX
FASHION DESIGNER

DOGS' NAMES: CAESAR BRITANNIC COX (LEFT) AND BRUTUS MAXIMUS COX (RIGHT)
BREED: ENGLISH BULLDOGS

I hadn't had a dog since I moved out of my parents' house in Canada when I was 16. I've always been drawn to English Bulldogs – even going so far as to have one star in perhaps my most iconic shoe ad from the 1990s. At the age of 46 I finally felt settled and mature enough to make the leap and got Caesar. What can I say? He is the love of my life. He is miserable and moody but I wouldn't have him any other way.

Then, two years later, I got Brutus. He's the polar opposite of Caesar. Even at six years old he's still a puppy – always happy and eternally with a ball in his mouth on the off chance you might want to throw it for him, they are unequivocally part of my life. My friends, my accountant, my solicitor and even my doctor know that if I am coming by my doggies will be in tow.

I shop in shops and eat in restaurants that allow dogs. (One can order Caesar Cox fishcakes from the doggy menu at George in Mayfair.)

My dogs have sat front row during London Fashion Week and have even accompanied me to the uber chic Serpentine Summer Party.

They have become the inspiration, the mascots and the logo for my new brand LATHBRIDGE.

PETE WICKS

REALITY TV STAR

DOGS' NAMES: **ERIC (LEFT) AND ERNEST (RIGHT)**
BREED: **FRENCH BULLDOGS**

If you could describe your dogs in three words, what would they be and why?
Handsome, mischievous and my best friends.

What is one of your first memories of your dogs?
My first memory of Ernest was when he met my mum's cat and he wanted to play with her. When she went for him, he ran and hid behind me like a big girl.

What's the naughtiest thing your dogs have ever done?
They once both decided it would be a great idea to escape from the garden and take themselves over to the park for a walk. I found them running around there like nutters.

Have any of your dogs ever had any diva moments?
Eric had a diva moment on the TOWIE photoshoot when he decided he had had enough and just went to sleep on set, mid shoot. I couldn't wake him up for love nor money. He was done and simply refused to do any more pictures.

What is the most cringeworthy 'oh no' moment?
The dogs refuse to let any woman sit near me on a bed or a sofa. They get in between us so that they get all the attention and if that doesn't work they tend to lick the woman non stop so she leaves me alone.

Which actor could provide your dogs a voice and why?
Ray Winstone would be Ernest and I think someone like Alan Carr would be Eric!

RICHARD ARNOLD
TELEVISION PRESENTER AND PERSONALITY

DOG'S NAME: **CLEMENTINE A.K.A. 'CLEMMIE'**
BREED: **COCKAPOO**

If you could describe your dog in three words, what would they be and why?
Not quite three words but my friend who took her for a walk one day described her as 'me on a leash'!

What is one of your first memories of your dog?
I announced on TV that I was going to pick up Clemmie from the breeder in Lancashire that first morning but when I got to Euston, there was a points failure at Milton Keynes and the train I was originally booked on was cancelled. I only had a small window to get there and back. Luckily the staff at Euston had seen me on TV that morning so they let me jump on another train with minutes to spare and told me to go get my girl! I arrived at Preston and fought through a fracking demonstration with my empty carry case – doggy bag I guess – and finally made it to the breeder just in time to pick her up. I was so nervous! Back we came on the train and tentatively she stepped out of the case and rested her head on my chest, looking up at me with those big brown eyes. Love at first sight!

Which actor could provide your dog a voice and why?
Which actor? Julie Walters!

RONAN KEATING

SINGER

DOG'S NAME: AUSSIE (SHE'S A GIRL)
BREED: PUG
AGE: TWENTY MONTHS OLD
FAVOURITE TOY: REX THE RACCOON

If you could describe your dog in three words, what would they be and why?
Friendly, cute and cheeky.

What is one of your first memories of your dog?
She was so cute when we first collected her from the breeder. She was so tiny she reminded me of a baked potato.

What's the naughtiest thing your dog has ever done?
Pooed on the carpet.

Has your dog ever had any diva moments?
If we left her alone in her pen for a couple of hours when she was a puppy she would turn her whole pen upside down and make a mighty mess in protest.

What is the most cringeworthy 'oh no' moment?
When she pooped in my manager's hand as a puppy.

Which actor could provide your dog a voice and why?
Rebel Wilson would voice her.

Noodle and Rosie

ROSIE FORTESCUE
REALITY TV STAR

DOG'S NAME: NOODLE
BREED: MINIATURE LONG-HAIRED DACHSHUND
AGE: 10 YEARS OLD

If you could describe your dog in three words, what would they be and why?
Three words to describe her would be loving, hungry and my world. She is literally the cutest, most affectionate little angel who loves food!

What is one of your first memories of your dog?
My first memory was being a teenager and coming home to Noodle after ten years of begging my parents for a dog. My twin sister and I were totally over the moon.

Has your dog ever had any diva moments?
She has diva moments when it comes to walking. She's not keen on pavements, only the park.

RUSSELL WATSON
SINGER

DOGS' NAMES: **BLAZE AND MUFFIN**
BREED: **BLAZE IS A GREYHOUND AND MUFFIN IS A SHIH TZU**

If you could describe your dogs in three words, what would they be and why?
My unconditional friends

What is one of your first memories of your dogs?
My Greyhound, Blaze, is a rescue dog. When he first arrived, he was completely lacking in any form of trust for anybody. It's been really lovely watching him develop into a trusting, loyal and loving family pet.

Muffin, my Shih Tzu, was a bundle of fun from the first moment I laid eyes on her. She still remains the same bundle of fun now!

What's the naughtiest thing your dogs have ever done?
There was one particular day that I had been searching everywhere for my mobile phone; I simply couldn't find it anywhere in the house. As a last resort I asked my wife Louise to ring it. She did so, only for us to discover that it was ringing from Muffin's dog basket. I think she had spent the last two hours thinking it was a bone. It still has the teeth marks on it. So every time I use it, it reminds me of Muffin.

Have your dogs ever had any diva moments?

Blaze, our Greyhound, is a complete diva. Whilst sat down he will often have his front paws crossed. My wife has purchased him a diamante dog collar, so you can imagine with his collar, paws crossed and nose in the air, it's quite a sight!

What is the most cringeworthy 'oh no' moment?

The most cringeworthy moment was with Blaze, our greyhound. Our alarm engineer had come round to service the system. Blaze managed to attach himself to his trousers. The chap promptly quipped, 'You don't need an alarm with him in the house.'

Which actor could provide one of your dogs a voice and why?

Blaze would probably be Hugh Grant, well-spoken and stereotypically British sounding, but also a little bit dithery.

RYAN GOSLING

ACTOR

DOG'S NAME: **GEORGE**
BREED: **GEORGE IS A BREED OF HIS OWN, HE'S ONE OF A KIND**

If you could describe your dog in three words, what would they be and why?
I can do it with one word... 'Enigma'.

What is one of your first memories of your dog?
One of my earliest memories of George is when he ate an entire tennis ball so I couldn't take it away from him any more. He won his very first battle and subsequently went on to win many great wars.

What's the naughtiest thing your dog has ever done?
The naughtiest thing would have to be the time he sneakily knocked over a few beer bottles at a BBQ, got a little drunk, relieved himself on a few people's legs, barked at those who wouldn't listen, said some things you can never take back and ultimately got us both thrown out of the place. In his defence, it was a pretty lame party and he was right that he was the only interesting dude there.

SALLY GUNNELL

OLYLMPIC GOLD MEDALIST
DOGS' NAMES: **BUMBLE AND DIGGIE**
BREED: **CHOCOLATE LABRADORS**

At the time of the pic I believe Bumble was three and Diggie was one. They are chocolate labs so pretty much all food is their favourite food! Bumble doesn't have a favourite toy but Diggie likes to carry around a teddy bear!

What's the naughtiest thing your dogs have ever done?
Bumble and Diggie learnt to open the old fridge door and ate the Christmas trifle, one year! The bowl was licked clean. It was only a small bit of cream that was on the end of their noses that gave them away!

Sasha and Lettice

SASHA WILKINS

LIBERTY LONDON GIRL

DOG'S NAME: **LETTICE**
BREED: **MINIATURE DACHSHUND**

If you could describe your dog in three words, what would they be and why?
Loyal (she has ridiculous levels of separation anxiety), loud (barks at EVERYONE and EVERYTHING), loved (I absolutely adore her, from her tiny paws to her silky ears).

What is one of your first memories of your dog?
When I met her the very first thing she tried to do was jump up onto my lap, which has remained her favourite place to be.

What's the naughtiest thing your dog has ever done?
Lettice is remarkably well behaved – she has no interest in chewing anything, or in stealing food. She did get stuck in the railings in Regent's Park last weekend; she slipped through them like a greased otter on the way in, chasing a squirrel, but then couldn't get back through. I don't love it when she chases and barks at much bigger dogs in the park. Given that she's only 3.5 kg she's going to get herself into a world of trouble one of these days.

Has the dog ever had any diva moments?
It's not really her style... unless you count (a) continuously refusing to accept anyone who works for me, even after a year, and doing low-level growling every time they walk into my office and (b) believing very much that the floor is an unacceptable option if I am around to carry her or pop her on my lap?

What is the most cringeworthy 'oh no' moment?
When she did a tiny poo right in the middle of a fashion showroom when I was busy talking to a designer. Mortifying.

Which actor could provide your dog's voice and why?
Someone petite with a surprisingly deep voice.

SUE PERKINS
COMEDIAN, BROADCASTER, ACTRESS AND WRITER

DOG'S NAME: **PICKLE**
BREED: **BEAGLE**

As a pup, you crunched every CD cover in the house for fun. You chewed through electrical cables and telephone wires. You ripped shoes and gobbled plastic. You ate my bedposts. As an adult you graduated to raiding fridges and picnics, you stole ice cream from the mouths of infants, you jumped onto Christmas tables laden with pudding and cake and blithely walked through them all, inhaling everything in your wake. You puked on everything decent I ever owned. You never came when called, never followed a path, never observed the green cross code and only sat on command when you could see either a cube of cheese or chicken in my hand (organic, or free-range at a push). I have said I love you to many people over many years; friends, family, lovers. Some you liked, some you didn't. But my love for you was different. It filled those spaces that words can't get to.

You were the peg on which I hung all the baggage that couldn't be named. You were the pure, innocent joy of grass and sky, and wind and sun. It was a love beyond the limits of patience, sense and commensuration. It was as nonsensical as it was boundless. You alchemist. You nightmare.

Thank you for walking alongside me during the hardest, weirdest, most extreme times of my life, and never loving me less for the poor choices I made and the ridiculous roads I took us down.

Excerpt from *Spectacles* by Sue Perkins

VIKKI STONE
COMEDIAN, ACTRESS AND MUSICIAN

DOG'S NAME: **BERT**
BREED: **SPRINGER SPANIEL**

If you could describe your dog in three words, what would they be and why?
Bert loves snacks. Snacks are his whole life and he is extremely snack motivated.
Sometimes he deliberately pretends to have something in his mouth he's not
meant to, just so he can be told to drop it, and get a treat.

What is one of your first memories of your dog?
Bert and Bill (our cat) meeting for the first time. Bill was very suspicious, and
rightly so. Bill's whole world changed that day.

What's the naughtiest thing your dog has ever done?
I have two dogs, Bert and Lily, who was from Dogs Trust Kenilworth, and she's
been with us now for a year. Over the course of the year, Bert and Lily have
taught each other their naughty tricks. For instance, Lily likes to pick up horse
poo, and run around with it in her mouth for a bit. Bert, who previously had no
interest in horse poo, now has a penchant for trotting around the fields with
horse poo in his mouth too, since we adopted Lily.

Lily wouldn't go near water, and then Bert taught her it was fun to play in the
stream, which was lovely, until one day, I look out the garden window, and see
Lily chest deep in the pond, trying to make friends with the goldfish, with a huge
grin on her face.

Has your dog ever had any diva moments?

Bert is a part-time show dog, and was in a tour show with me a couple of years ago. His starring role was running through a tunnel, doing a couple of dance moves, and trotting through the audience at the end of the show. One particular night, he decided to run out the tunnel, and instead of his usual dance moves, slowly drag his bum along the floor as a choir sang behind him. The audience fell about laughing, as there was no stopping him, it felt like it went on for ages. He was dragging his bum along the floor and that was that.

What is the most cringeworthy 'oh no' moment?

We were filming an advert together, and Bert was VERY excited. So excited that his 'lipstick' was out the whole time they were trying to film him, and it wouldn't go down even after making the whole crew wait twenty minutes. In the end, the on-set, vet had to make him less excited with a bottle of water. I still cringe when I think about it now!

Which actor could provide your dog a voice and why?

Bert won't need to be voiced by an actor, because one day he will talk. I know it. I'm currently trying to teach him how to sing, and he does sing along with the piano, so watch this space for Bert's debut album!

LEAH WELLER

MUSIC ARTIST, MODEL AND DJ
DOG'S NAME: **LUNA**
AGE: **2 YEARS OLD**
BREED: **LONG-HAIRED CHIHUAHUA**

If you could describe your dog in three words, what would they be and why?
Cheeky, loving and loyal.

What is one of your first memories of your dog?
The first memory of Luna was when we brought her back home for the first time and she was a puppy so she kept falling asleep sitting up.

What's the naughtiest thing your dog has ever done?
Luna likes to steal food and objects that cost a lot, so she does naughty things on a daily basis but never gets told off because of her ability to make you feel bad for her with her cute face.

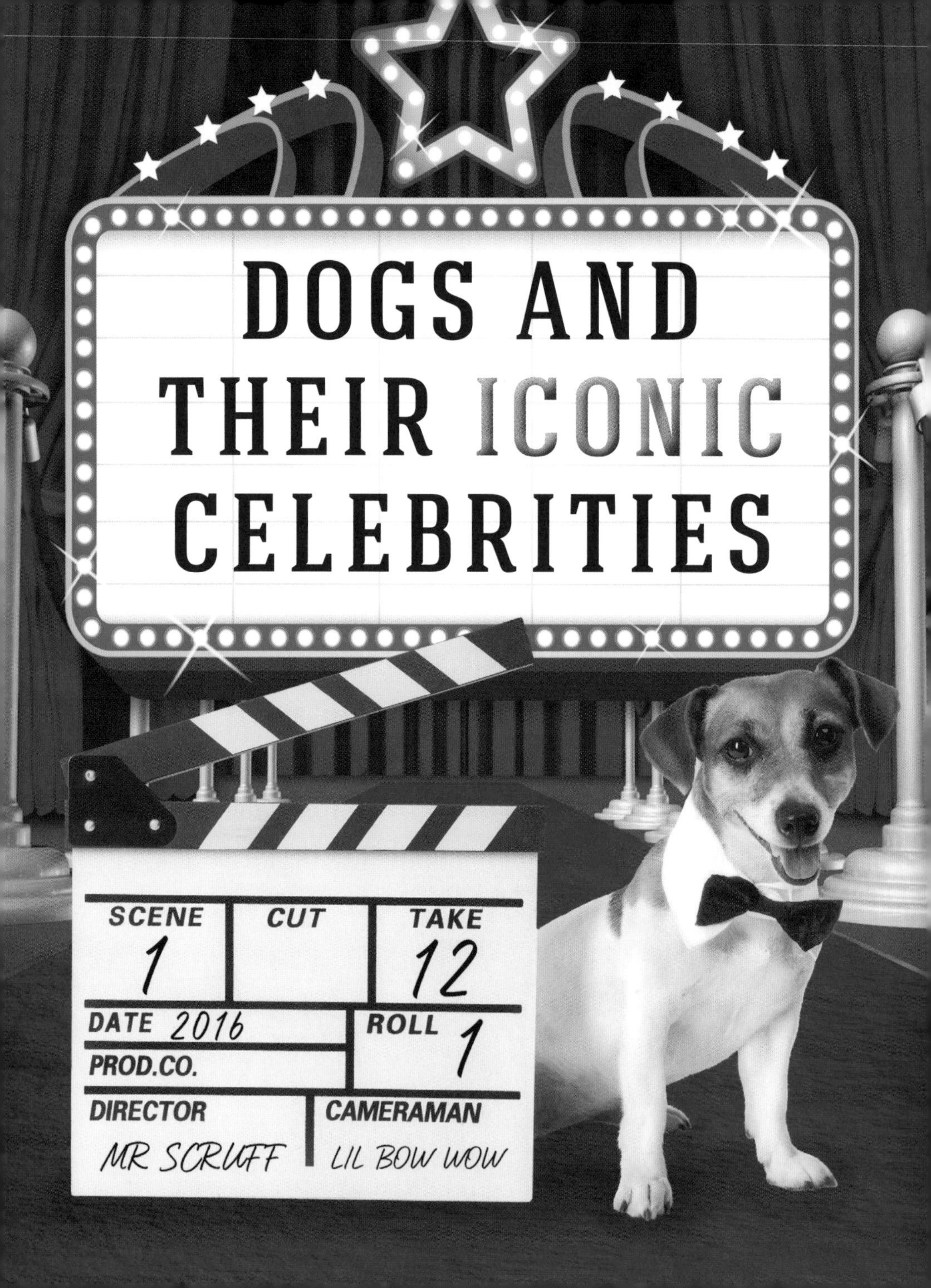
DOGS AND THEIR ICONIC CELEBRITIES
SCENE 1
CUT
TAKE 12
DATE 2016
ROLL 1
PROD.CO.
DIRECTOR MR SCRUFF
CAMERAMAN LIL BOW WOW

MARILYN MONROE

ACTRESS, MODEL AND SINGER

1962

JOHN WAYNE
ACTOR
AND WIFE, ESPERANZA BAUR,
AND HIS DOGS, FEARLESS
AND STAGECOACH
1947

AUDREY HEPBURN
ACTRESS
AND HER YORKSHIRE TERRIER,
MR FAMOUS
1947

JEAN SIMMONS
ACTRESS
WITH HER DOG, BESS
1952

LAUREN BACALL AND HUMPHREY BOGART

ACTRESS   ACTOR

1947

ELIZABETH TAYLOR
ACTRESS
1954

SOPHIA LOREN
ACTRESS
WITH HER POODLE
PUPPY, TIM
1965

JUDY GARLAND
ACTRESS AND SINGER
1937

GRACE KELLY
ACTRESS AND MODEL
1954

DogsTrust

125 YEARS OF SAVING DOGS' LIVES 1891-2016

Huge thanks for buying this book – you have just helped us to care for thousands of stray and abandoned dogs! ALL the royalties from the sale of *Dogs and their Faithful Celebrities* will come straight to Dogs Trust. Dogs Trust is the UK's largest dog welfare charity, caring for around 17,000 dogs per year, through our network of 20 rehoming centres. Crucially, we NEVER put a healthy dog to sleep. Our non-destruction policy is just one of the things that makes us stand apart from the crowd. We care for dogs of all ages, shapes and sizes, and thanks to the kindness of people like you, we will be able to continue to save more dog's lives.

Did you know we also work hard to prevent dogs from going stray or being abandoned at all? We offer low cost neutering operations and microchipping for dogs, and offer free school talks for children all around the country. If you would like to find out more about our work, how you can rehome a dog from us or where your nearest rehoming centre is, please visit **www.dogstrust.org.uk**.

Thank you!